BRITISH ISSUES

WATER

Jillian Powell

FRANKLIN WATTS
LONDON • SYDNEY

First published in 2007 by Franklin Watts
338 Euston Road, London NW1 3BH

Franklin Watts Australia
Level 17/207 Kent Street
Sydney NSW 2000

Copyright © Franklin Watts 2007

Editor: Julia Bird
Designer: Thomas Keenes
Picture researcher: Sarah Smithies

Picture credits:
Agripicture Images, Alamy: 12. Bob
Richardson, Alamy: 27. epa, Corbis: 13. Geoff
Tompkinson, Science Photo Library: 20. ©
Gideon Mendel/Corbis: 5. Graham Mulrooney,
Photographer's Direct: 23. HIP, TopFoto: 6.
Image Source, Corbis:11. John Prior Images,
Alamy: Contents. John Prior Images, Alamy:
24. Jon Sparks, Alamy: 19. Martine Hamilton
Knight, Arcaid: 28. Pat Bennett, Alamy: 18.
Patrick Eden, Alamy: 17. Playboy Archive,
Corbis: 10. Rex Features: 21. Sakchai Lalit, AP,
PA Photos: 29. Sang Tan, AP, PA Photos: 14.
Skyscan, Science Photo Library: 16. Steve
Austin, Papilio, Corbis: 8-9. Thames Water: 15.
Tim Cuff, Alamy: 22. Topfoto: 25. Waterwise:
26.

A CIP catalogue record for this book
is available from the British Library

ISBN: 978 0 7496 7605 6

Dewey Classification: 333.91'0941

Printed in China

Franklin Watts is a division of
Hachette Children's Books,
an Hachette Livre UK company.

CONTENTS

DESERT OR FLOOD?

In Britain, water has become a hot news topic. Emergency drought orders, floods, water pollution and rising water charges all regularly make the headlines. Many people predict that water shortages will be one of the main issues affecting our lives in the 21st century.

Drought...

Although Britain is widely seen as a rainy country, below average rainfall and a dense population mean that the south-east region now has less water available than the desert countries of Egypt and Sudan. Groundwater sources and reservoirs are at their lowest levels for decades.

...And flood

While water companies in the south-east impose emergency drought orders and hosepipe bans, reservoirs in the west country and Wales sometimes have to release water to prevent flooding. Sudden, heavy rainfall and snow can make rivers burst their banks across Britain.

Changing climate

The climate in Britain is changing due to global warming. Scientists studying climate change predict that summer rainfall in Britain will fall by 20 per cent by the 2080s. At the same time, they also predict more violent storms and floods. Five million people in Britain already live in flood risk areas, and average damages from flooding cost us over £1 billion every year. Heavy rainfall can restore groundwater levels over time, but it can also saturate the ground so quickly that it causes run-off, flooding and pollution, which can adversely affect water supplies.

Why water matters

Changing weather patterns, a growing population's demand for water and the need to protect the environment are making water a topical issue around the world. The actions we take now will have a major impact on the future of water in Britain.

▶ In July 2007, torrential rain resulted in devastating floods across Britain. The River Severn burst its banks in Gloucestershire, leaving local towns and fields under metres of muddy water.

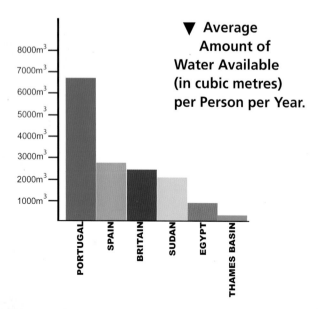

▼ Average Amount of Water Available (in cubic metres) per Person per Year.

8000m³
7000m³
6000m³
5000m³
4000m³
3000m³
2000m³
1000m³

PORTUGAL · SPAIN · BRITAIN · SUDAN · EGYPT · THAMES BASIN

THE WATER INDUSTRY

Up until the early 19th century, water for drinking, washing and industry came straight from rivers, springs and wells. There were no main drains and sewers, so rivers were badly polluted with sewage and carried deadly infectious diseases, such as cholera and typhoid.

Victorian engineering

The 'Great Stink' from the River Thames in London became so bad during the hot summer of 1858 that Parliament rushed through laws to build sewers under the city. Doctors had recently realised the importance of sanitation to health, and engineers began to design and build a system of pipes and pumping stations to carry clean water to Britain's towns and cities. Many of these Victorian mains and pipes are still in use today.

▼ This cartoon, dating from 1858, shows Death rowing past dead dogs and rubbish on the filthy River Thames in London.

JUST THE FACTS

- The Environment Agency and the Scottish Environment Protection Agency are responsible for water resources and flood defences.

- The Consumer Council for Water represents customers in England and Wales and investigates complaints.

- Ofwat and The Water Industry Commission for Scotland monitor water companies' charges and encourage efficiency and competition in the industry.

- The National Rivers Authority is responsible for pollution and flood control regulations.

- The Drinking Water Inspectorate (England and Wales) and Drinking Water Quality Regulator (Scotland) monitor the quality of drinking water.

Water works

Today, the water industry supplies over 20 million homes. It collects, treats and supplies about 16 billion litres of water a day. It also collects and treats more than ten billion litres of waste water a day. To do all this, the water industry maintains 1,000 reservoirs, over 2,500 water treatment works, 9,000 sewage treatment works, and over 700,000 kilometres of mains and sewers – enough to stretch to the Moon and back!

Water bodies

Since the Water Act of 1989, water in England and Wales has been controlled by ten private water and sewerage companies. They have to meet the water quality

Up for discussion

The Water Act of 1989 allowed parts of the British water industry to be passed from the government to the private sector (known as privatisation). Do you think that the water industry should be in the hands of private companies? What do you think might be some of the advantages and disadvantages of this?

▼ Private Water Companies in Britain.

standards set by British and European Union (EU) laws. In Scotland and Northern Ireland, water and sewerage are provided by two government-owned companies – Scottish Water and Northern Ireland Water.

WATER SUPPLY

The water in our taps comes from rainfall or melted snow. Although Britain is wetter than many parts of the world, the high population density means that the amount of water available per person is lower than in many far drier countries.

Rain variation

Rainfall in Britain is also unevenly distributed. The most rain falls in the more thinly populated north and west of the country, and the least in the crowded south-east region, which has the highest demand for water.

Water sources

About 67 per cent of British water comes from rivers, lakes, springs and wells (surface water), while 33 per cent comes from underground aquifers (groundwater). Groundwater has to be pumped out through wells or deep boreholes that are drilled into the rock. This is done in areas where the underlying rock is porous (such as chalk or sandstone) and water collects in sponge-like aquifers underground. Most of this groundwater comes from sources in central, eastern and southern England.

Boreholes drilled to create the Channel Tunnel were taken over by Thames Water to supply its treatment works at East Ham. The nine boreholes supply about 20 million litres of groundwater a day to 120,000 customers in Barking and East Ham.

Water treatment

Water is carried by pipes to Britain's treatment plants. Here it has to go through a series of processes to make it safe to drink.

Clarification – chemicals are added to make any pollutants float or sink.
Filtration – small debris or particles are filtered out.
Disinfection – chlorine is added to kill bacteria. Fluoride may also be added to protect against tooth decay.

The clean water is then pumped through large plastic pipes called trunk mains to a water tower or underground reservoir. From here, it travels through smaller mains into a network of pipes in our towns and cities. This network feeds the taps in people's homes. In some areas, it can take up to a week for water to travel from the treatment plants to homes.

◄ Most Scottish water comes from surface water like this stream. This makes it very vulnerable to changes in weather and climate.

HOUSEHOLD WATER

▲ Standard showers use less water than baths, but modern power showers can use up more water than a bath in just five minutes.

JUST THE FACTS

Shower = 5 litres per minute

Flushing toilet = up to 9.5 litres

Bath = 80 litres

Washing machine = 80–120 litres

Washing car with hose = 400 litres

Garden sprinkler = 1,000 litres of water per hour

About two-thirds of Britain's water is used by households. On average, each person uses about 160 litres of water a day for drinking, cooking and washing. This compares to just ten litres used by many people in developing countries in Asia, Africa and South America.

Rising consumption

Over the last ten years, water use in Britain has increased by seven per cent or ten extra litres per person per day. Overall, water consumption has increased by a staggering 70 per cent in the last 30 years. In England and Wales, water companies predict that our demand for household water will rise by a further 12 per cent over the next 25 years.

How we use our water

We use about a third of our water for personal washing, such as showers, baths, hand washing and cleaning teeth. A third is used for flushing toilets, and the rest is used for washing clothes, cooking, dishwashing, washing cars and watering gardens. Many modern homes have water-hungry appliances and gadgets such as dishwashers, combi-boilers, power showers, jet sprays for washing cars or patios and hosepipes or sprinklers for watering gardens.

▶ Washing a car with a bucket and sponge uses much less water than using a hose.

Up for discussion

Why do you think we are using so much more water than before?

Which uses should take priority in a water shortage?

What could be done to make the global water situation fairer?

INDUSTRY AND AGRICULTURE

About a third of the water consumed in Britain is used for industry and farming. Industry consumes 1300 million cubic metres a year, with food and drink, electronics and chemical manufacture consuming the most.

Industrial use

Almost every manufacturing industry uses water for steam production, cooling towers, washing and other production processes, while a water-cooled power station can use up to 230 million litres of water per hour. The food, brewing, chemical and pharmaceutical industries are all heavy users of water, too. Water is also used extensively by the leisure industry for swimming pools, golf courses and theme parks. Watering a golf course for one day can use enough water to supply 1,000 households.

► Spray irrigation is being used for a water-hungry potato crop on this farm.

Water wise

The British government and various environmental groups are putting pressure on businesses to carry out water audits, then set targets for water efficiency and reduction of waste. At the moment, a laundry uses around 80 million litres of water a day, and a hospital can consume up to 200 million litres. Studies suggest that between 25 per cent and 75 per cent of water could be saved by taking straightforward measures, such as detecting and repairing any leaks and replacing or upgrading old equipment.

Agriculture

Water is used in farming to irrigate crops and fields, and for livestock upkeep. Since the 1970s, the amount of water used for irrigation has been increasing. This is partly because we are growing more water-dependent crops, such as potatoes and sugar beet. British farmers are now being encouraged to replace spraying with drip irrigation or low-pressure sprinklers to reduce water wastage, and to grow more low-irrigation crops such as carrots, cabbages and beetroot. Global warming is already affecting farming further south in Europe, where drought has halved wheat and maize harvests.

Embedded water

Everything we buy and use contains 'embedded water'. This is the water that has been used during the manufacture of the product – for irrigation, cooling, washing or other production processes. Around 65 per cent of embedded water is found in food and drink, but household products such as clothes, and industrial goods such as cars, also contain large amounts of it. The government is encouraging consumers to think more carefully about the amount of embedded water in goods, particularly food and drink, that they buy, and to buy more water-efficient goods where possible.

▼ The textile industry uses thousands of litres of water at each stage of production.

JUST THE FACTS

Amount of embedded water used in the production of:

1 tonne of steel = 100,000 litres

1 kg of cotton = 5,300 litres

1 kg of rice = 200 litres of water

1 kg of potatoes = 500 litres

1 portion of chips = 25 litres

1 magazine = 9 litres

1 bar of chocolate (100g) = 1 litre

THE COST OF WATER

One of the hottest debates about water is how much it should cost us. Since the water companies were privatised in 1989, they have had a duty to make profits for their shareholders as well as providing a service to their customers.

Foreign investors

Increasingly, Britain's water companies are being bought by large overseas companies. High-profile examples include Britain's biggest water company, Thames Water, which was bought by an Australian bank for £8 billion in 2006. Many of these investors have been criticised for raising water charges while failing to invest enough in new mains and pipes.

▲ The headquarters of Thames Water in Reading. Thames Water has been the focus of debate during droughts in the south-east.

Rising charges

In 2005, the average daily cost for household water was 68 pence. While the cost of water in Britain remains relatively cheap (in developing countries, people can pay on average twelve times more), water charges are rising. In the south-east they have gone up by almost 25 per cent in the past two years. At the same time however, customers are increasingly likely to face hosepipe bans and other restrictions on their water use during times of drought.

Investment

Water companies justify price hikes by pointing out that, by 2010, they will have spent £5.5 billion to improve drinking water and protect the environment in England and Wales. Many people believe that more investment is needed to replace or repair mains and pipe networks. Investment targets are set by the Water Services Regulation Authority (Ofwat) in England and Wales and the Water Industry Commission for Scotland. They have the power to impose fines if companies fail to meet targets to control leakages.

Faulty pipes

Many of Britain's water mains and pipes were laid in Victorian times and are now over 100 years old. Extreme weather can cause these pipes to burst and leak. Almost 25 per cent of total water supply is lost from the water companies' networks through faulty pipes and leaks – enough to supply ten million households!

CASE STUDY
London's water

Over 60 per cent of Thames Water's mains in London are over 100 years old. The company has already replaced over 600 kilometres of old cast-iron pipes with more flexible plastic ones, and plans to invest £500 million to replace a further 1,600 kilometres of mains in the next five years. On this timescale, it would take another 100 years to replace the entire network.

▼ Thames Water workers replace old water pipes in London's Piccadilly area.

Up for discussion

Should we be prepared to pay more for our water?

Should we all pay the same for our water, or should the south-east region pay more?

Is it right for overseas companies to own and run Britain's water supplies?

A GROWING GAP

There is a growing gap between the amount of water available in Britain and the amount we use every day. If current trends continue, water use will increase by 40 per cent over the next 20 years.

Growing demand

Demand for water is growing, due to natural population increase and a social trend towards both smaller households and more people living alone. The government predicts that the British population will increase by 2.8 million by 2016, and estimates that 3.3 million more households will be created. In the south-east, they are proposing to build over half a million new homes by 2025, increasing water demand in the comparatively dry region still further. A recent report by the Institution of Civil Engineers predicts

▼ Lifestyle changes and a growing population, bolstered by immigration from other EU countries, has led to increasing demand for housing and water in Britain.

Up for discussion

If the south-east is suffering water shortages now, should the government be building more homes there, increasing demand?

Should we all be made to have water meters to control demand?

a shortage of up to one billion litres of water a day in the south-east region of Britain by 2031.

Weather and rainfall patterns

The amount of water available for use is falling, due to new laws protecting water in the environment, and changing rainfall and weather patterns. The European Union Habitats Directive (1992) and the Environment Agency's Water Act (2003) have introduced restrictions on the amount of water that can be abstracted (taken out) of groundwater or rivers. This is necessary to protect valuable wetlands and wildlife.

Loss of groundwater

Groundwater is increasingly at risk from pollution. Poor water quality has led to the closure of 146 groundwater sources in the last 30 years, resulting in a loss of 425,000 cubic metres a day – enough to supply nearly three million people. Groundwater

can be polluted by pesticides and chemicals used in farming or industry, and by run-off and overflowing sewers during heavy rain and flooding.

Compulsory metering

One way to control water use is making water meters compulsory. Currently, householders without a meter are charged a standard rate for water, based on the size of their property. Water meters can help customers to keep track of their consumption, and trials have shown that they can reduce household use of water by around ten per cent. New homes and re-builds already have meters, accounting for one in four households. The government plans to draw up a map of water-stressed areas by 2009, as the basis for a compulsory metering scheme.

◀ Water meters record the quantity of water used and charge customers accordingly.

CASE STUDY
Compulsory meters

In 2006, the government Department for Environment, Food and Rural Affairs (DEFRA) granted the Folkestone and Dover Water Services 'an area of water scarcity' status. This gave the water company the right to install compulsory metering in 90 per cent of their customers' homes by 2015. They predict a fall of 10–15 per cent in consumption as customers pay for water as they use it.

WATER AND THE ENVIRONMENT

Britain's rivers, lakes and coastal waters are protected by the Environment Agency and the Scottish Environment Protection Agency (SEPA). These organisations enforce laws set by the EU Water Framework Directive, which came into force in 2000. It introduced laws to protect Britain's waters and restore them to health by 2015.

Diffuse pollution

The environment agencies work with the water companies to clean up pollution. They have to meet EU standards for water quality and clean beaches. Every year, there are thousands of incidents of water pollution in Britain. Water can be polluted by sewage, chemicals used in fertilisers or pesticides for arable farms, livestock units and fish farms, and industrial waste. These pollutants can seep through soil into groundwater, or run off into rivers and lakes. This is called 'diffuse pollution'. New measures are being taken to reduce it, such as controlling the use of fertilisers in sensitive areas, and leaving chemical-free margins around arable land. However, chemicals can also leak from storage tanks or landfill sites, or pollute water through accidental spillages.

◀ This river in Cheshire has been polluted by an oil spill, which is contaminating the water and endangering local wildlife.

Sewage

Sewage is another pollutant of inland and coastal waters. About 75 per cent of sewage goes through sewage treatment works run by the water companies, while the rest is treated in septic tanks or is directly discharged into rivers, streams and the sea. Water can also be polluted by run-off from roads, transport and car washes. Storms and floods can increase run-off and cause sewers to overflow, leading to pollution of groundwater.

Abstraction of water

The Environment Agency and SEPA also have a responsibility to control the amount of water that is abstracted (taken out) from the environment. Wetlands are rich habitats for wildlife, and they also help to soak up and filter storm water and run-off from roads. Wetlands are also a natural weapon against global warming, as they absorb carbon dioxide. But many have been drained for agriculture or development, or become polluted by sewage, acid rain and chemicals used in

farming or industry. Others have been over-exploited for leisure use or resources such as peat. The government is now supporting the Environment Agency and SEPA's efforts to protect wetlands. Some 167 sites, covering 9,000 hectares of British wetlands are now officially protected, while the Wallasea Island wetlands project in Essex has created one of the largest protected wetland areas in Europe.

▲ A flock of lapwings at Leighton Moss wetland nature reserve in Lancashire. Birds and other wildlife populations can be endangered by water pollution.

Up for discussion

Who should pay for the clean-up of polluted water?

How can we balance our demand for water against the needs of wildlife and the environment?

CASE STUDY
Protecting wildlife

If river levels fall too low, fish and other forms of wildlife, including birds and otters, are at risk. In the summer of 2006, the Environment Agency had to pump groundwater into the River Itchen near Southampton to raise the river level, as salmon were unable to swim upstream to breed.

DRINKING WATER

Health scares, and the marketing of branded water as trendy and healthy, have led to a growing market for bottled water in Britain. Every year, we drink over two billion litres, spending around £700 million in the process. The market for bottled water is predicted to keep growing at nine per cent every year for the next five years.

Drinking water quality

In Britain, the water from our taps is tested for safety and quality by the Drinking Water Inspectorate in England and Wales and the Scottish Drinking Water Quality Regulator in Scotland. They monitor the practice of the water companies and carry out tests at water treatment works, distribution systems and taps. They also investigate complaints and incidents. Poor practice, accidents and freak weather conditions such as storms and floods can lead to water being contaminated by bacteria, such as E. Coli. However, tap water met strict quality standards in 99.96 per cent of cases in 2005.

▶ Water samples are tested for bacteria in laboratories. Bacteria can be responsible for water-borne diseases such as typhoid and cholera.

▲ Attractive design and packaging can be key factors in making people buy branded mineral water.

Costs of bottled water

In spite of this, more and more people are buying bottled water, although it costs on average 10,000 times more, litre for litre, than tap water. Bottled water also has high environmental costs. Some producers are accused of disrupting water supplies in local communities, leading to water shortages. There are also high costs in terms of energy use in manufacturing, packaging and transport. Most bottles are made from plastic and end up in landfill sites, where they take hundreds of years to biodegrade (rot away), or are burnt in incinerators. Only ten per cent of bottles are recycled, and over half of these are sent to China to be processed, producing yet more greenhouse gases on the way.

JUST THE FACTS

● Around 154 billion litres of bottled water are consumed globally every year.

● In Britain, one in five bottles comes from water sources abroad.

● The bottled water industry produces around 33,200 tonnes of carbon emissions every year.

● The manufacture of PET plastic bottles uses 0.25 per cent of global oil consumption every year.

● The first biodegradable plastic bottles came on the market in 2006.

Up for discussion

Why do we buy bottled water when the environmental costs are so high?

How much should we be prepared to pay for safe drinking water?

CLIMATE CHANGE

In Britain, we are already feeling the effects of global warming. Our summers are generally getting warmer and drier, while winters are overall becoming milder and wetter. Monthly rainfall is regularly falling below average. Global warming is also bringing more severe storms, with strong winds and seasonal flooding. Since 1998, flooding has caused over 40 deaths in Britain.

England and Wales

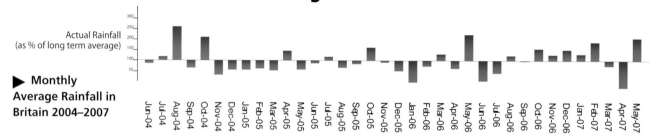

Actual Rainfall (as % of long term average)

▶ Monthly Average Rainfall in Britain 2004–2007

Impact on water supply

Global warming will mean that there is less water available, due to changing rainfall patterns and more frequent droughts. When it is hotter and drier, we tend to use more water for our gardens and outdoor activities, thereby increasing demand. Seasonal flooding can also disrupt supplies. In July 2007, a water treatment plant in Gloucestershire was flooded, leaving an estimated 350,000 homes without water.

Water quality

Climate change can also affect water quality. Violent storms lead to sewer overflows, polluting groundwater. Waterworks may be lost or damaged

◀ Global warming is predicted to lead to rising sea levels and more violent storms.

CASE STUDY
Falling river levels

The River Pang, believed to be the river in Kenneth Grahame's famous novel *The Wind in the Willows*, begins in the Berkshire Downs and runs into the River Thames at Pangbourne. By the spring of 2006, it had lost a third of its water due to low rainfall levels. This has had a dramatic impact on local populations of insects and other wildlife.

▶ The River Pang in Berkshire.

due to coastal erosion and rising sea levels. Britain is also getting more heavy storm rains, and these tend to run off into rivers and other surface water rather than recharge groundwater. Rising sea levels may also lead to a loss of groundwater in coastal areas, as seawater can flow into aquifers and mix with the fresh water.

Drought in the south-east

The area of Britain most affected by falling rainfall levels is the south-east. The eleven million people who live in the region get their water mostly from boreholes that tap into chalk aquifers. Two dry winters in 2004–5 reduced the water available by 30 per cent. Some predict that by the 2080s, summer rainfall in the region may have fallen by up to 50 per cent.

Coping with climate change

The water industry is a large energy user, and contributes around three per cent of British greenhouse gas emissions (the leading cause of global warming). It is working to use more renewable energy sources, which currently make up under nine per cent of its total energy use. The industry is also making long-term water resource plans to cope with climate change. These include building more reservoirs to capture winter rain, improving sewer design standards to cope with increases in storm run-off and planning for new or replacement water treatment works.

CASE STUDY
Flood risk

In June and July 2007, days of torrential rain led to disastrous flooding across England and Wales. Thousands of people had to be evacuated from their homes across the worst-hit areas and local power and water supplies were cut off. The total cost of the flood damage was estimated at around £2 billion.

PLANNING FOR THE FUTURE

As Britain's water problems increase, the water companies are drawing up 25-year plans to ease shortages. As well as putting forward proposals for saving water and reducing waste, they are looking at schemes to increase available supplies.

New reservoirs

One proposal is to build more reservoirs, but this is costly and can take up to 20 years from design to completion. Suitable sites are hard to find and can meet local planning opposition. In low-lying areas, water has to be pumped from a nearby river but this uses a lot of energy, creating greenhouse gases, and few rivers have reliable enough volumes of water. Some reservoirs could be extended by raising dam walls. In the next 25 years, five new reservoirs and three extensions to existing dams are proposed in England and Wales.

▼ The dam at Craig Goch reservoir in Powys, Wales.

▶ This desalination plant in Dubai produces over 270 million litres of water a day.

Desalination plants

In dry regions like the Gulf States, desalination plants provide up to 60 per cent of water supplies. These turn salt water into drinkable water by drawing it from the sea and pushing it at high pressure through filters. Minerals are added and the water is disinfected. Desalination is reliable and technology is improving, but the water is expensive (about 60–100 pence per cubic metre) and uses high amounts of energy, creating around 25,000 tonnes of greenhouse gases a year. Desalination technology also produces large amounts of salt waste. Two plants are proposed for England and Wales in the next 25 years.

Should Britain have a water grid?

Many people believe that Britain should have a water grid. This would distribute water around the country, by pumping it from areas with higher rainfall to the drought-hit south-east. However, a report by the Environment Agency in 2006 suggested a grid would be costly, environmentally damaging, and use too much energy, creating greenhouse gases. Another proposal is to bring in bulk supplies of water by tanker from Scotland, or by ship from Norway.

CASE STUDY
Beckton plant

Thames Water are proposing to build a £200 million desalination plant at Beckton, on the north bank of the Thames. By 2009, it would supply 140 million litres a day – enough for 400,000 homes. However, the proposal was blocked by the Mayor of London, Ken Livingstone, who argued that the plant would be unsustainable and would add to global warming. He pointed out that Thames Water should work instead on mending its pipes, which currently leak a third of all water they transport.

Up for discussion

Should Britain have a water grid to distribute supplies around the country?

Why might the construction of new reservoirs meet opposition from local people?

SAVING WATER

There are many ways to reduce the amount of water we use at home. These include switching to low-water appliances, recycling grey water, and changing the ways we use water for everyday tasks.

Being Waterwise

Waterwise is an independent organisation that has been set up and funded by the water companies. It is campaigning to reduce our individual consumption of water by 25 litres a day by 2010. Waterwise awards their marque (right) to water-efficient appliances and promotes ways of saving water every day, such as turning taps off when brushing teeth, not over-filling kettles or pans and mending dripping taps. Water companies are also taking their own measures to reduce demand, such as sending out water-saving advice with bills and holding roadshows. Anyone can attend these roadshows, where they will receive tips on saving water and can buy water-saving products, such as rainwater butts.

▲ The Waterwise marque tells customers which appliances are most water efficient.

JUST THE FACTS

- Running taps use about eight litres of water a minute.

- Dripping taps can waste four litres of water a day.

- Washing a mug under a running tap uses about a litre of water.

- Taking a bath uses a third more water than a five minute shower – but power showers can use more!

Low-water appliances

Modern household appliances, such as washing machines and dishwashers, are becoming more water efficient. If used correctly, some dishwashers actually use less water than hand washing. Washing machines can recycle rinsing water, or use ultrasonic agitation to clean clothes more efficiently with less water. Modern toilets have short flushes, and using a save-a-flush device in the cistern can reduce the amount of water used further. Air shower devices can be fitted to power showerheads. They work by filling droplets with air to reduce flow by a third.

Grey water

Grey water is the water waste from our sinks, baths and showers. It can be collected through a recycling system and treated so that it is suitable for flushing toilets. Using grey water, we could each save 18,000 litres of water a year, or a third of our daily household water.

Saving water outdoors

We can save water outdoors by growing plants that are drought-resistant, and by using rainwater butts or grey water to water the garden.

▶ Plants with light-reflecting leaves, like this Jerusalem Sage, can withstand drought.

CASE STUDY
Millennium water

'Watercycle' was a grey water-recycling scheme set up for the Millennium Dome. It supplied up to 500 cubic metres of water per day (more than half the total demand) for toilet flushing using recycled grey water.

NEW TECHNOLOGY

Globally, scientists are looking at new solutions to bridge the gap between supply of and demand for water. These include rainwater harvesting, the recycling of grey water or sewage and the 'seeding' of rainclouds.

Rainwater harvesting

In the home, rainwater can be collected to save up to 50 per cent of household water. Harvesting systems can be installed in homes to collect rain from roofs and driveways and store it in underground tanks. This water can be filtered and used for toilets, washing machines and garden watering. It requires separate piping from mains water, and a control unit to monitor tank levels, so that if supplies drop, customers can switch to the mains supply.

▼ Jubilee Campus at Nottingham University was the world's first environmentally friendly campus. It includes a series of lakes to collect rainwater run-off and cool the university buildings.

Recycling sewage

New technology has introduced schemes to treat and recycle sewage and waste water. The waste has to go through a series

of processes to remove viruses and chemicals such as phosphates, nitrates and ammonia. After treatment, it can be pumped back into waterways.

▲ During a prolonged drought in Thailand in 2005, 'Cloud Attacker' planes like this one released rain-making particles into the clouds in an attempt to bring rain.

Cloud seeding

To seed rainclouds, aircraft fly into the lower atmosphere and drop particles of dry ice or silver iodide. These particles attract moisture in the cloud, forming droplets that become larger, then fall as rain. Cloud seeding is already practised in over 20 countries worldwide, most notably in drought-stricken regions of China. However, it produces only very localised rainfall so is not a suitable solution for large dry areas.

CASE STUDY
Using waste water

At Langford in Essex, there is an award-winning scheme for sewage recycling. Essex and Suffolk Water draw sewage and waste water from the Chelmsford Treatment Works for cleansing and recycling. The treated water is pumped back into the River Chelmer for abstraction at Langford.

JUST THE FACTS

● By 2025, global use of water is predicted to rise by 40 per cent.

● A third of the world's people currently face water stress, which is defined as access to less than 1000 cubic metres of water per person per year. This is predicted to rise to over half the world's population in the next 25 years.

GLOSSARY

Acid rain Rain that has been polluted by chemicals from cars and industry.

Aquifers Underground beds of earth, gravel or porous rock that contain stores of water.

Atmosphere The mass of air surrounding the Earth.

Audit A studied examination of a company's accounts.

Boreholes Holes that are drilled deep into the ground to reach water.

Coastal erosion A wearing away of coastal land by pressure from the sea

Desalination plants Treatment works for removing salt from seawater to provide drinkable water.

Diffuse pollution Pollution through various sources.

Drought A long period of time with no rainfall.

Embedded water The water that is used when something is produced.

Emergency drought orders Powers for the water companies to impose restrictions on water use during times of drought.

Global warming A warming of the planet's climate, believed to be caused by carbon emissions from cars and industry.

Greenhouse gases Chemicals in the air, such as carbon dioxide and methane, that contribute to global warming. They are known as greenhouse gases because they trap warmth in the Earth's atmosphere like the inside of a greenhouse.

Grey water Water that has been used and can be recycled for flushing toilets or watering gardens.

Groundwater Water beneath the surface of the ground.

Infectious Easily spread from one person to another.

Pharmaceutical Drugs and medicines.

Population density The number of people relative to the size of the area they live in. High population density means many people live in a small area; low population density means a small number live in a large area.

Porous Allowing water and air to pass through it.

Renewable energy A source of energy that does not run out and is constantly renewed, such as wind or solar power.

Run-off Water that runs off land during storms or heavy rains.

Sanitation Facilities that promote hygiene and prevent disease spreading, such as sewage disposal and rubbish collection.

Shareholders People who own shares in a company. They are entitled to a part of the company's profits.

Surface water Water on the Earth's surface, in rivers, streams, lakes, seas and oceans.

Ultrasonic agitation Using ultrasonic waves to 'shake' clothes clean.

Victorian Dating from the reign of Queen Victoria (1837–1901).

Water mains The principal pipe in a network of pipes, usually underground.

FURTHER INFO

Books

21st Century Debates: Water Supply, Rob Bowden (Hodder Wayland, 2002)
Global Issues: Water under Threat, Larbi Bouquerra (Zed Books, 2006)
Dealing with Waste: Waste Water, Sally Morgan (Franklin Watts, 2006)
Down the Drain: Conserving Water, Anita Ganeri and C.Oxlade (Heinemann Library, 2005)
Disasters in Nature: Drought, Catherine Chambers (Heinemann Library, 2001)
Improving our Environment: Saving Water, Jen Green (Hodder Wayland, 2006)

Information

www.ccwater.org.uk
The website for the Consumer Council for water, representing water consumers in England and Wales.

www.defra.gov.uk
The website for the British government department in charge of the environment, food and rural affairs.

www.environment-agency.gov.uk
The website for the body responsible for protecting the environment in England and Wales, with sections on water resources and water quality.

www.ofwat.gov.uk
The website for the economic regulator for water and sewerage services in England and Wales, with a section on water-saving tips.

ww.sepa.org.uk
The website for the Scottish Environment Protection Agency.

www.water.org.uk
The website for Britain's water industry, with lots of water facts and information.

www.waterwatchscotland.org
The website for the body that represents water customers and investigates complaints in Scotland.

Practical action

www.savetherain.info
The website for a campaign to conserve rainwater.

www.waterwise.org.uk
The website for a non-profit organisation supported by the water companies dedicated to saving water.

www.wwf.org.uk
The website for the Worldwide Fund for Nature in Britain, with an A to Z of water saving tips.

www.wwt.org.uk
Website for the Wildfowl and Wetlands Trust – a conservation organisation that works to protect wetlands and their wildlife.

Note to parents and teachers: Every effort has been made by the Publishers to ensure that these websites are suitable for children, that they are of the highest educational value, and that they contain no inappropriate or offensive material. However, because of the nature of the Internet, it is impossible to guarantee that the contents of these sites will not be altered. We strongly advise that Internet access is supervised by a responsible adult.

INDEX

These are the lists of contents for each title in *British Issues:*

Future Energy
The importance of energy • The state of energy today • Declining fossil fuels • Climate change • The nuclear debate • Wind power • Water power • Power from the Sun • Power from the Earth • Energy from waste • Innovations • Saving energy • Government and citizen action

Population Change
Britain's changing faces • Measuring change • People in the past • Population at work • Changing families • New lifestyles • Life moves • Trading places • Immigrants and emigrants • The European Union • Cultural identity • Ageing population • Looking to the future

Sporting Success
2012 • A rich history • Governing bodies •Funding • Facilities • Sport and society • The business of sport • Success stories • Sport and education • Fair play • Sport and the media • Sport and national pride • Looking towards 2012

Sustainable Cities
What does it mean to be a sustainable city? • Urban versus rural populations • Planning sustainable cities • Urban regeneration • Issues in the south-east • Stuck in the city • City movers • Sustainable energy • Water • Dealing with waste • Urban wildlife • Cities of opportunity • Vision of the future

Waste and Recycling
What is waste? • Throwaway society • What happens to waste? • Why waste matters • Managing waste • Reduce and reuse • Recycle! • How recycling happens • Composting • Energy from waste • Why don't we recycle more? • Changing the rules • A way to go

Water
Desert Britain? • The water industry • Water supply • Household water • Industry and agriculture • A growing gap • Climate change • The cost of water • Saving water • Drinking water • Water and the environment • Planning for the future • New technology

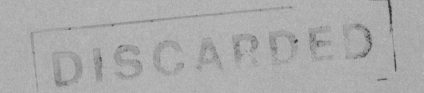